For Nikki

Gerald Escapes To Mars

Copyright © 2021 Lucas J Machado
All rights reserved. No part of this book may be used or reproduced in any manner whatsoever without written permission except in the case of brief quotation embodied in critical articles and reviews.

Written And Illustrated by Lucas Machado
www.lucasmachado.art

ISBN: 978-1-7362788-4-0 (paperback)

First edition

GERALD ESCAPES TO MARS

Lucas Machado

Gerald's parents were always nagging him to brush his teeth, clean his room, and do his chores.

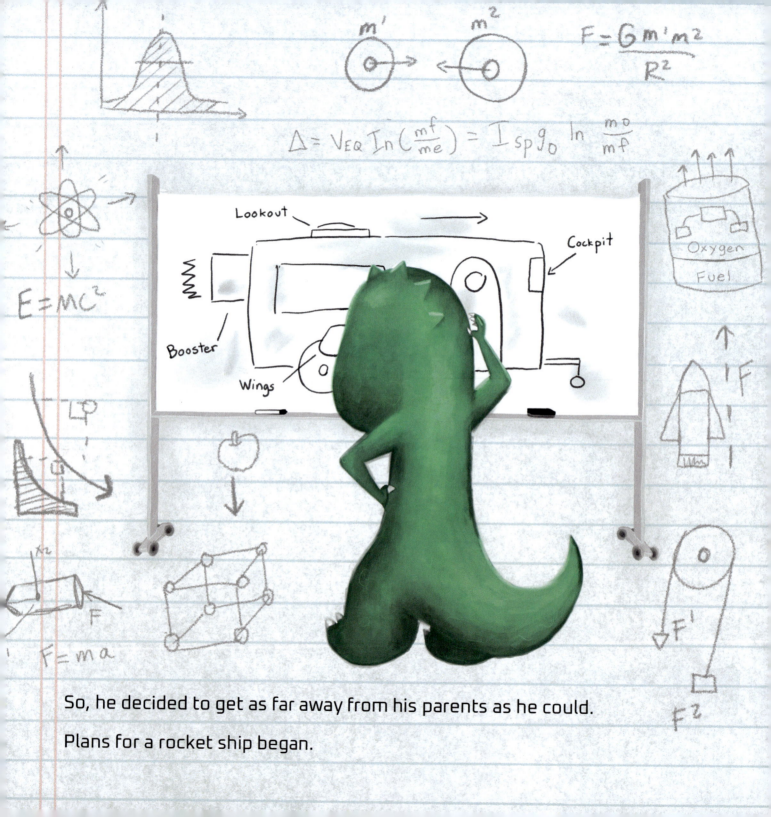

So, he decided to get as far away from his parents as he could.

Plans for a rocket ship began.

Gerald's little sister, Sally, joined the crew. "We are going to live on Mars," said Gerald, "we can do whatever we want on Mars."

The family camper became the rocket's cabin.

An old surfboard was perfect for the wings.

They even made spacesuits.

You can't breathe on Mars, so they had to pack their own air.

Lots of food was needed too. They decided fruits and vegetables were too heavy.

Finally, the rocket ship was ready.

Oh no! Sally forgot to pack her blankie.

There was only ten seconds left before takeoff.

Gerald had to think fast.

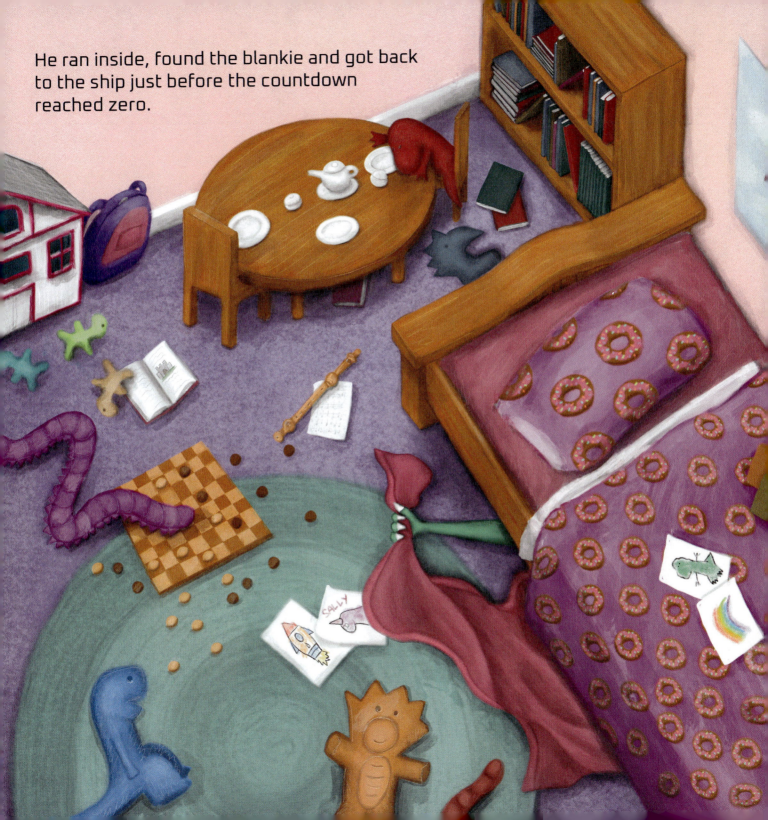
He ran inside, found the blankie and got back to the ship just before the countdown reached zero.

The rocketship launched. They blasted out of the neighborhood, zoomed past the moon and soared all the way to Mars.

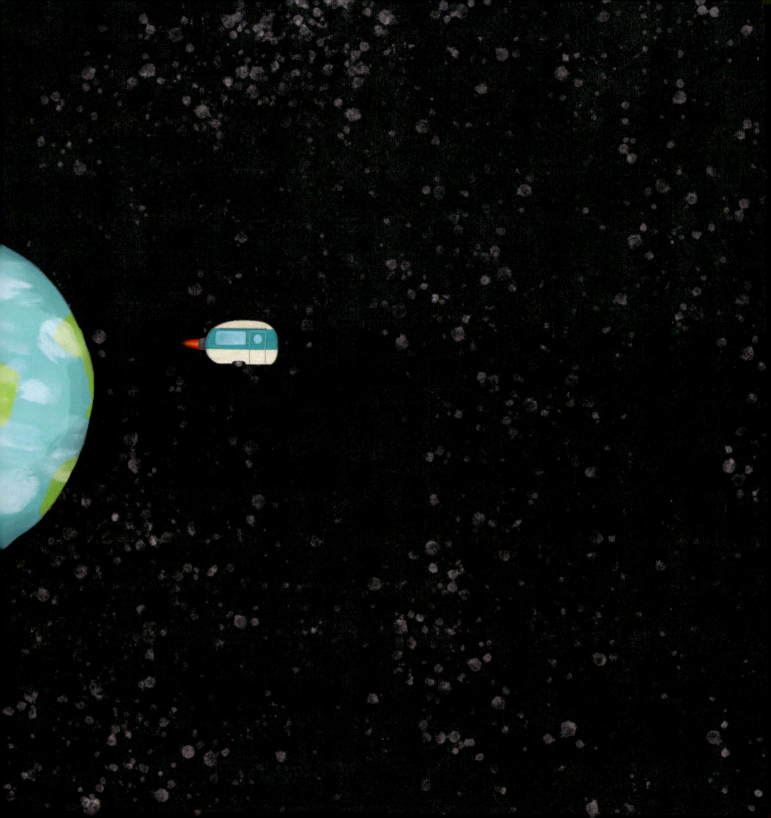

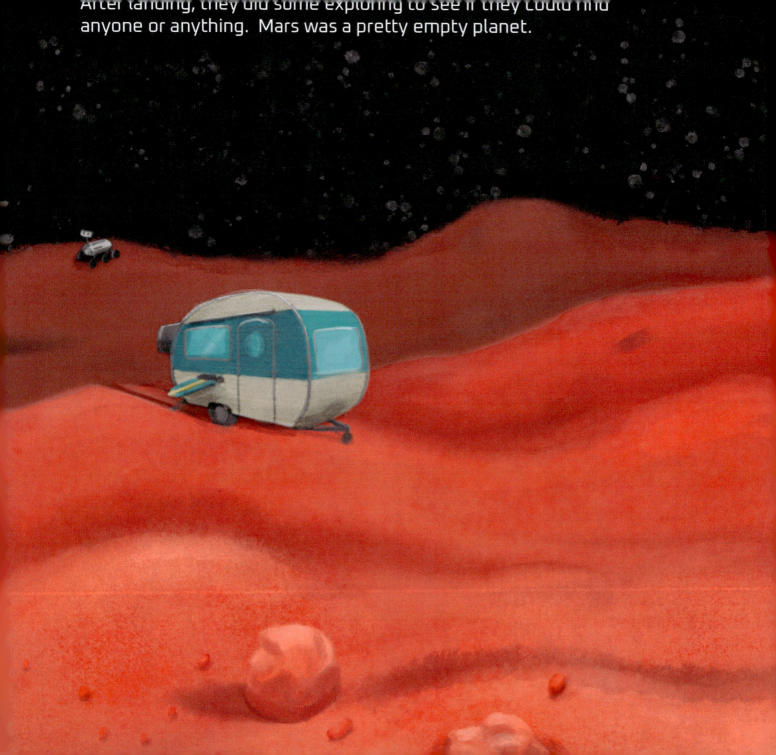

After landing, they did some exploring to see if they could find anyone or anything. Mars was a pretty empty planet.

Eventually, they found a new friend!

His name was Rover.

They had lots of fun together.

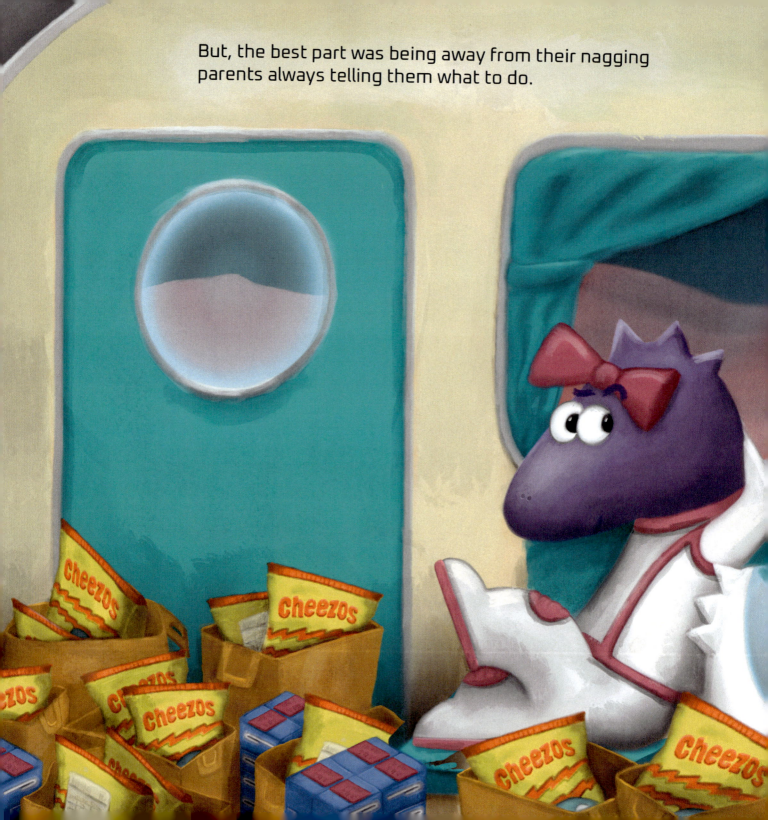

But, the best part was being away from their nagging parents always telling them what to do.

There were a lot of snacks.

There was a lot of screen time.

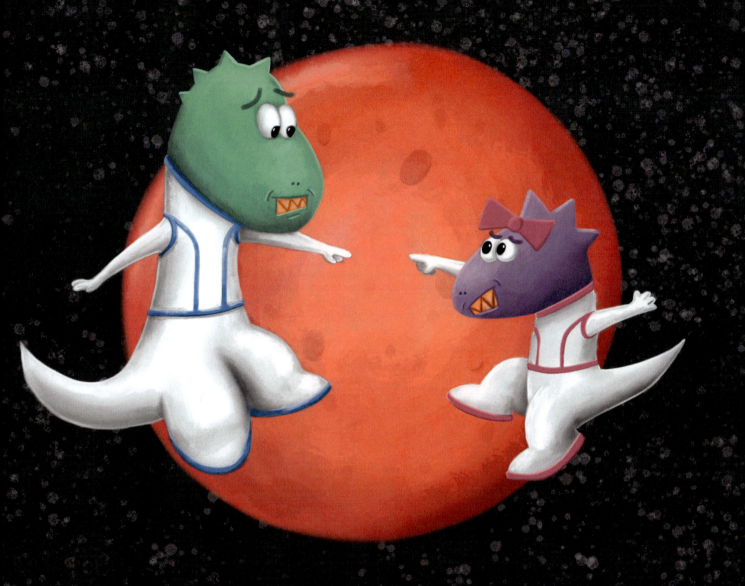

"And look at our teeth," he continued, "They're all orange!"

So they made a chore chart with all the jobs that needed to be done.

The rocket ship was cleaned up...

and the teeth were brushed.

But the messes kept coming.

"This is a lot of work," said Gerald, "At home, we didn't have to do all the chores."

Also, the air they brought was almost all gone.

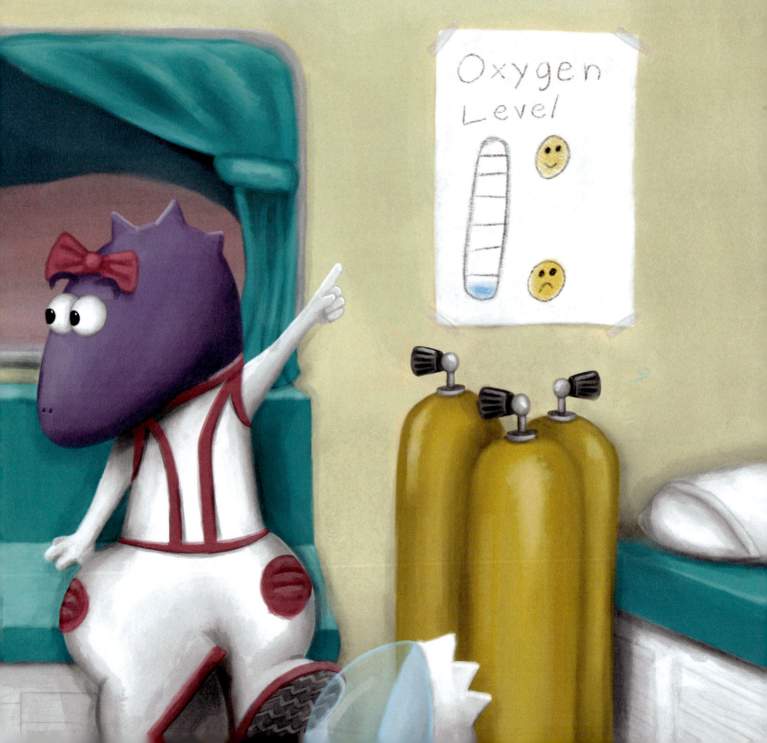

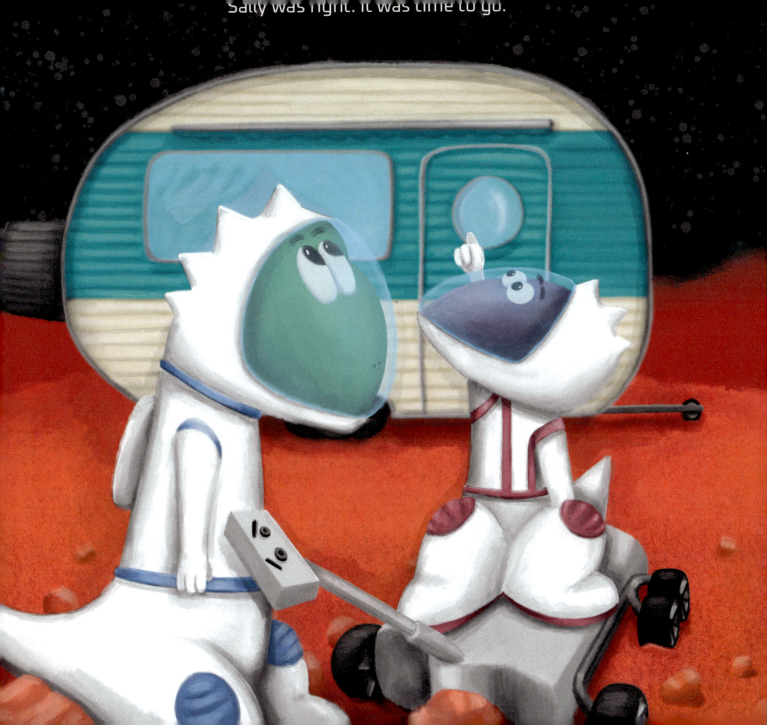

Sally was right. It was time to go.

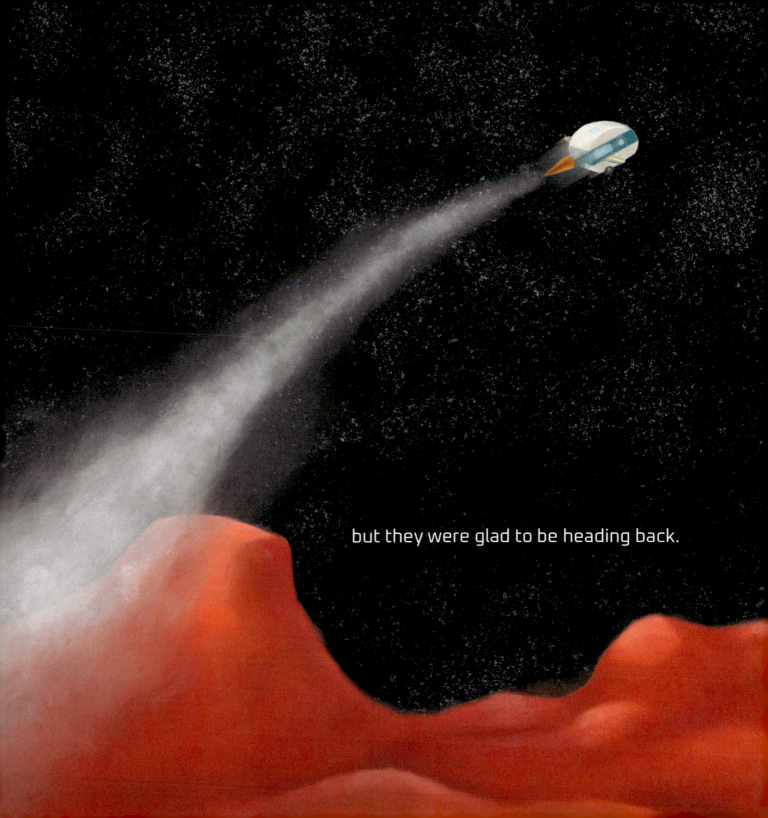
but they were glad to be heading back.

However, their adventure was not over yet.

After flying back to Earth, the rocket ship was going so fast the wings broke off.

They were heading straight for a crash with their own house!

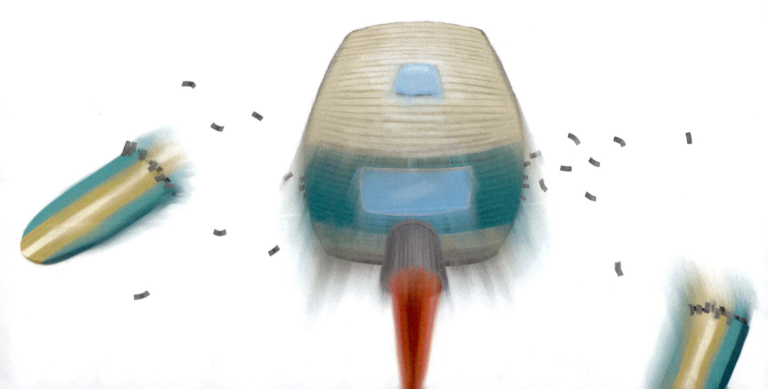

Sally put her blankie over her head.

That gave Gerald an idea.

It was worth a try.

The blankie parachute made for a soft landing.

Finally home, they jumped into the arms of Mom and Dad.

That night, Gerald and Sally brushed their teeth and did their chores without being reminded even once.

What would you bring if you took a trip to Mars?

What would you need to live?

What about for fun?

What else?

Give Gerald and Sally five stars on Amazon!

Check out more books at
www.LucasMachado.art

How To Draw Gerald

Now add your own idea

A hat?   A jetpack?   Baseball?

How To Draw Sally

Now add your own idea

An Apple?   Helipack?   Trampoline?

Made in the USA
Las Vegas, NV
05 December 2023